LESSONS

SIMPLE WORDS THAT MATTER

Inspiring Stories to Reinforce Life's Most Teachable Moments

by Rick Tocquigny

Life Lessons…Simple Words That Matter

Copyright 2011 Rick Tocquigny

*Published by Simple Truths, 1952 McDowell Road,
Suite 300, Naperville, Illinois 60563*

Simple Truths is a registered trademark.

Printed and bound in the United States of America.

ISBN 978-1-60810-120-7

*www.simpletruths.com
Toll Free 800-900-3427*

Book Design: Vieceli Design Company, West Dundee, Illinois

01 WOZ 11

TABLE OF CONTENTS

PREFACE

Life is a series of circumstances, events and experiences. I'm a firm believer that life is about gaining perspective through learning moments and turning those into teachable moments for those we influence. These moments become the key to our own learning and "life lessons."

So what are the key life lessons that influence each person today? In my opinion, it's about having a strong foundation, developing best practices, and living by a core value system that drives your intentions, decisions and actions.

Here are the top six essentials that I've learned and which I continue to try and apply 365 days a year:

Lean on your faith

Love and honor your family and cherish your friends

Live with intention through core values

Know your strengths and maximize them

Surround yourself with the right people

Strive to live a balanced life

What are the top best practices that are essential to you? I encourage you to write them down and review them often. What we absorb tends to be what we become. Who we surround ourselves with tends to be who we become. And how we live our life tends to be how we treat others.

Above all else, learn and embrace life lessons and let them be a road map that leads to living life through mission, vision and a passionate pursuit. *Be inspired and inspire others!*

Troy Johnson

INTRODUCTION

The art of telling life's lessons was taught by my mom and dad…all my life. With the passing of these two great storytellers, a chasm was created. Now taking on their role, this book embodies the spirit of their storytelling. As this book shares lessons, I encourage you to share your own stories within your family and communities, carrying your own history forward into a "lessons learned legacy." As my dad said,

> "Learning from experience is a faculty that should always be practiced."

Inside *Life Lessons-Simple Words that Matter* are profound stories made up of simple, but powerful truths. Rich, indeed, is the person who has heard and applied words of wisdom, maxims, proverbs, short stories and common sense anecdotes to guide his or her life. Through simple words, we bring forth universal truths, setting us on a course for more enlightened living.

Life Lessons-Simple Words that Matter is a contemporary philosophy which embodies a purposeful approach to sharing stories. My hope is to start a renaissance of face-to-face conversations centered on life's teachable moments.

From Life Lesson's radio (www.blogtalkradio.com) and the hundreds of guests, bloggers and super-charged fans, I have been the recipient of many lessons. The experience has strengthened my view to seek the greatest good in all humans, envisioning a culture where lessons are learned and shared.

At the end of every story we conclude with "above all else." You will find a clear take-away moral to every short story and lesson. It's our "get it-got it" approach.

And above all else, with the writing of this book come many prayers that you will start sharing your own life lessons beginning with your family, friends, neighbors, work colleagues and your community at large. *May your life lessons be an encouragement and a teachable moment to every person who chooses to listen.* By all means, tell your own lessons about how God has worked in your life and how special milestone moments indelibly shaped and formed you. Share life lessons at your own pace, pass on your wisdom and enjoy your passionate journey.

"As iron sharpens iron, so one person sharpens another." — PROVERBS 27:17 NIV

Remember, great transformations simply take a great amount of time. Talking about life lessons is a healthy part of life. It builds character, integrity and a value system that is irreplaceable.

In appreciation,

Rick Tocquigny

ACKNOWLEDGEMENTS

There are many talented people that helped complete this book and set the stage for a life lessons movement. First and always foremost, to my wife and best friend of 33 years, Carla—for her support, patience and innate ability to organize and shape my language into an "enjoyable read."

To my literary agent and friend, Jonathan Clements, for his tenacity, executive-producer vision and network that continues to build our Life Lessons Radio show content excellence.

To Troy Johnson, for his thought leadership and belief in this project. I consider his "orbiting" skills in the industry as among the very best.

To Mac Anderson, Founder and President of Simple Truths, for his vision and mission behind changing lives with the written word. He is a great source of encouragement.

To my daughters, Heather and Jennifer, for fueling the need to stay relevant, use an economy of words and think creatively "off the grid."

To the editorial and creative team at Simple Truths for their intelligent approach and drive for excellence with this book.

DEDICATION

This book of life lessons is dedicated to my parents, George and Petie Tocquigny. They took the time to make a lasting impression on my life with storytelling, enriching my life with wisdom, adventure and wit. Their simple words matter most and made an indelible difference to all that knew them.

"Consider that each lesson is like a paving brick. When woven together they form a beautiful path for you to walk, share with others and an avenue for the next generation."

—PETIE TOCQUIGNY

Life's Lesson #

No
Pockets

*In the final chapters of one's life, wisdom
settles in comfortably like a favorite hat,
a good friend or even an old pillow. It just
seems to fit well and make sense.*

Taking time to visit with an old friend, Hattie Kunz told me that her acquaintance in Austria had passed away and was buried in a white linen shirt. I leaned in to listen very carefully. Hattie's stories always captivated me.

"I thought it was really odd to be buried in a plain white shirt with no pockets."

Her friend, Frederick, was a very determined, self-made millionaire. Having worked all his life, he built a successful career as an industrialist following World War II. As a survivor of the Great Depression, followed by years of prosperity, Frederick had reached a level of wealth and prominence known to few men.

"The world breaks everyone and afterward many are strong at the broken places."

— ERNEST HEMINGWAY...*A FAREWELL TO ARMS*

But there he lay in the walnut coffin, dignified yet humbly dressed. "I suppose it seems reasonable that he should dress as a simple man considering he is going before God Almighty, but the thing is Frederick was known for his extravagant displays of wealth." It had occurred to Hattie at that very clarifying moment:

You simply can't take your treasures with you. He had no pockets.

Of all the lessons to learn at age 80.

Hattie had spent her life saving, proudly overcoming poverty, raising a family, only to wake one day and find her children grown and her husband dead. She was left with a fortune, but now it all felt meaningless. Standing in front of Frederick, she now saw the world differently. What had she missed? All of this time spent accumulating wealth, but not caring for the needy, even the needy within her own family.

Since her profound life lesson occurred, Hattie did a little research on burial clothing. She went on to tell me about Rabbi Simeon Gamliel who lived 200 years after Christ's death and resurrection.

> *Understanding his own imminent death, the good Rabbi requested the use of a simple shroud as his burial clothing, just like Jesus'.*

She explained that the use of shrouds protected the very poorest from embarrassment at not being able to afford lavish burial clothing. Since shrouds do not have pockets, the Rabbi was able to get across one final message that wealth and status cannot be acknowledged or expressed in death.

Upon Hattie's return home, she started seeing opportunities to give to the needy. And yes, she has even made the decision to be buried in a humble shroud without pockets. She also decided on a very simple coffin. ***"In the end, the deceased really don't appreciate fine furniture and the savings can go to my church and community who really need the help."***

Life Lesson...

Above all else:

YOU HAVE A LOT TO GIVE,

regardless of your age
or stage of life.

ALWAYS LOOK FOR
BETTER
WAYS

*T*he year was 1963 and third-year coach of the young Dallas Cowboys, Tom Landry, looked for a better way to recruit talent. Using the most sophisticated IBM computer, Landry could work with 80 different football skill variables. His assistant coaches had given him 300 variables to consider.

Tom had learned from his coaching mentors at the New York Giants. **He took the 300 variables and transformed them into a language** that college coaches and scouts could comprehend. Narrowing down to five tangibles, Landry formulated key words that defined his selection process;

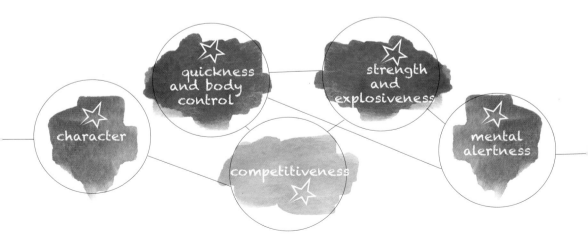

Since players' weight, height, and speed in the 100-yard dash were measurable, Tom did no further evaluation with these statistics.

The thought for this systematic approach started in 1960, the Cowboys' inaugural season. Along with Gil Brandt, their talent coordinator, and Tex Schramm, the General Manager, the computer-aided draft forever changed the face of the recruiting process.

There was always a sense of urgency to find a better way. In 1961 they chose Don Meredith of SMU for his quick, accurate arm, flashy and fluid style—attributes that were not included in their first IBM program.

"The will to win is important, but the will to prepare is vital."

— JOE PATERNO, COACHED PENN ST. TO 400 VICTORIES

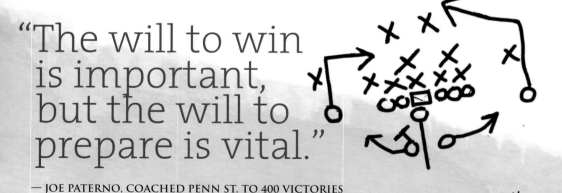

BROWN RIGHT 34

Meredith, who passed away in 2010, was a rare sort, both as an athlete and as a humorous person. He was a friendly guy from Mount Vernon, Texas, just 100 miles east of Dallas. He was an All-State basketball player, 4-H State Champion in shrub judging, star of a one-act play competition, and class president. Somewhere along his journey, he picked up the nickname of "Dandy Don."

To Coach Landry, Don Meredith didn't seem well prepared, at least not by his standards. Landry realized how casual Meredith was in their first blackboard session.

"I felt like the village fool," Meredith recalled. "All of my life even numbers had been to the right and odd numbers to the left. In Coach Landry's system, it was just the opposite. I had never called formations using colors.

"Tom would draw a play…say brown right, 34, which means the fullback carries to the left. Then he'd erase it and ask me to draw it. By then I was twitching all over. At SMU we just lined up in a spread, I got the ball and threw or ran. We never attacked a defense. It never occurred to me that it made any difference in what the defense was doing. But that was the whole thing in the Cowboy system. *It took me three years to learn how much study and dedication are necessary to be a pro quarterback.*"

As the Cowboy draft system unfolded, it became a competitive tool that separated the Dallas franchise from other clubs. Future Hall of Famer Mel Renfro was in the freshman class for this system. Scoring high on the five key intangibles, Renfro was a cinch first-round choice in Landry's eyes until November 22, 1963, that fateful day when President John F. Kennedy was assassinated in Dallas. With his normal intensity, Mel had built himself to a peak for his Oregon Duck finale against arch-enemy Oregon State. When he learned that the game was postponed, his anger combined with sadness peaked as he rammed his fist through a plate glass window at his residence.

The initial reports alarmed Landry, learning that Mel Renfro had severed a nerve and lost feeling in his thumb. All teams passed on him in the draft until Landry confirmed that Mel would be okay. The Cowboys eventually snagged him in the second round. In the years to follow, **Mel Renfro became "the standard" with a proven Cowboy draft system.**

And that following year, the system brought forth Bullet Bob Hayes, two-time Olympic Gold medal track star, future All-Pros Ralph Neely and Jethro Pugh, along with the incomparable South Carolina halfback Dan Reeves, the eventual head coach of the Denver Broncos and Atlanta Falcons.

Life Lesson...

Above all else:

You can always
IMPROVE YOUR TEAM WITH SUPPORTIVE SYSTEMS,

but the intangibles of character and competitiveness must be regarded as critical to a winning program.

SISTERHOOD
THROUGH
THICK AND
THIN

*"Is solace anywhere more comforting than
in the arms of a sister?"*

— ALICE WALKER

A wise woman said, ***"Once sisters are grown, it becomes the strongest
relationship."*** Veronica and Angela Cartwright, popular actors of film and
television, have thrived as sisters helping each evolve as family, professionals
and friends. Even though the partitions of blue and pink once separated their
childhood bedrooms, they always had each other's back. Simply put:

Helping one another was and
remains the backbone of the
Cartwright sisterhood.

The Cartwright family moved from Bristol, England, via Canada to Los
Angeles, California, in search of a better life. In fact, it was Mrs. Margaret
Cartwright's dream to live by the sea, ideally to a warmer climate than
Bristol. Without any clear intention of pursuing show business, Margaret

Cartwright learned of the Lola Moore modeling agency from a neighbor. Lola found immediate opportunities for both daughters, Veronica (6½ years old) and Angela (3 ½ years old).

Veronica became the face for Kellogg's cereal gracing television commercials and box tops. She was cast in a number of popular movies such as *The Children's Hour*, *Spencer's Mountain*, and Alfred Hitchcock's *The Birds*. Veronica also performed in four different roles on *Leave it To Beaver* including Violet, the first girl to kiss the "Beaver." She also starred as Jemima Boone in *The Daniel Boone Show*. She was featured in the movies *Alien*, *The Witches of Eastwick*, *The Right Stuff* and more recently, the TV series *Eastwick*.

Angela vaulted into our living rooms as Danny Thomas' stepdaughter, Linda Williams, on *Make Room for Daddy*. She then starred as Brigitta Von Trapp in *The Sound of Music,* followed by a starring role in television's *Lost in Space* as Penny Robinson. She has appeared in TV movies and established herself in the art world by authoring three books, including *Mixed Emulsions*.

Along the way, acting never got in the way of sisterhood.

"We built thick skins as individuals and supported each other as actresses," noted Angela. "You have to be in each other's court, always be ready with helpful tips, and add a difference to each others' lives."

It was important to be resilient, especially since you could not count on winning every role at every audition. ***Thick skin and mental toughness were two key ingredients.***

One sunny day that "thick skin" experienced a different sort of test. It all happened during a priceless time of imaginative play as children. Having received Annie Oakley outfits with the fringed dress, gun and holster, the girls created their own backyard horse-riding stable. With Veronica as the trainer and Angela playing the horse, they would practice their jumps and hurdles. On that fateful day, Angela slipped and skinned her chin. Mom patched her up, Veronica took the scolding and the Danny Thomas' show

"A sister is a little bit of childhood that can never be lost."

— MARION C. GARRETTY

writers altered the script to include a reason for the skinned-up face. Still bearing a tiny scar from that horse play, Angela claims that, *"You simply learn to pick yourself up, brush yourself off and keep going."*

As the girls grew up, their taste in colors and fads varied. Showing their individuality, Veronica decorated her room in avocado and white with Andy Warhol-style posters. Wearing avocado-green dresses and shoes as often as possible was also a part of "Veronica's way." "This was the way I wanted to do things," said Veronica. "It was a time of finding yourself and being different."

Angela preferred the bright colors and the psychedelic look of *Yellow Submarine* and Peter Maxx. Her room sported a hot-pink carpet with orange accents.

The accumulation of those precious, colorful stories is what makes sisterhood substantial. And it's not just the stories that frame Veronica and Angela's personal experiences, *they have built a friendship around the simple act of living, listening and encouraging each other through the ups and downs of being children, teenagers, young women, adults and parents.*

The destination for these two sisters is happiness. For the Cartwrights, *everything comes from knowing that you have taken the time to stay*

emotionally connected. When you choose to sustain sisterhood, you make the time to meet, you allow happiness to catch you; you maintain tradition and you are present to bring joy. With sisterhood comes mutual respect, open-mindedness and a lifetime of knowing what makes each other tick. "A working Veronica is a happy Veronica" exemplifies how Angela deeply understands her sister's rhythm.

And because life is not perfect, loved ones pass away and sometimes move on. *There is nothing sweeter and more comforting than the sound of a sister's voice in the season of sorrow.* Angela and Veronica have also managed to have substantial influence in the lives of their own offspring. By intentionally living in close proximity, they can inspire the next generation and enlarge the past traditions of the Cartwright family.

Life Lesson…

Above all else:

Sisters support each other
THROUGH THICK OR THIN.
Investing yourself in these relationships
allows the true self to emerge,
whenever, however.

Life's Lesson # **4**

BURN THE
UNDERBRUSH...

*Success May Be On the
Other Side Waiting for You*

"Always do more than is required of you."
— FIVE-STAR GENERAL GEORGE S. PATTON

*I*n your life of work, you will hit phases when you know that promotion, raise or special goal is within your reach, yet you grow disgruntled and impatient. When you have worked hard to build a body of work, but you feel like throwing in the towel, consider that true success may be right around the corner.

At this very moment in time, it is hard to see the big picture, orbit above all the action and understand your progress.

Remember the legend of a general who found his troops disenchanted, disparaged and whipped. He believed that it was because his army division felt isolated and endangered by the enemy. The general knew that his division was physically close to other regimens, separated only

"Be strong and do not give up, for your work will be rewarded."

— 2 CHRONICLES 15:7 NIV

by a dense growth of small trees and shrubbery. To lift his troops' spirits and let them see the might of the vast army, he then ordered *"burn the underbrush."*

When his explicit orders had been carried out, his division of soldiers found that they were not isolated, as they had supposed. To their surprise, they saw that they were a part of one mighty army approaching near victory. *With their courage revived, they marched forward in triumph!*

Life Lesson...

Above all else:

Consider where you have been, what you have accomplished in your body of work and burn the brushwood of self-doubt, over-eagerness, mistrust, and separation.

YOUR SUCCESS MAY BE MUCH CLOSER THAN YOU EVER CONSIDERED.

Life's Lesson # **5**

THE RIGHT
MOUNTAIN

> *"Most of the shadows of this life are caused by*
> *our standing in our own sunshine."*
>
> — RALPH WALDO EMERSON

In 1988, Jim Hayhurst, a 47-year-old former Procter & Gamble professional and advertising executive, became the oldest member of the Canadian Expedition to reach the summit of the tallest peak on earth, Mount Everest. The 29,028 foot journey is a riveting story (www.therightmountain.com) filled with life-threatening experiences that forever changed Jim's life.

In this all too formulaic world where we seek quick solutions, easier paths to get from point A to point B in our lives, and answers to soothe our own wounds about career, marriage and relationships, Jim's climb to the summit is his individual story, but it can be yours, too. **The secret to using lessons is to apply the learning in a personal, individual, unforced manner.** The experience of age is about finding the best lessons that build your own layers of wisdom and looking at the shadows that people cast upon themselves.

LESSON ONE:

Take on the world in bite-sized pieces.

Early on in the acclimatization trek for Everest, Jim realized that he and his Canadian Expedition colleagues were facing a 120-mile walk and climb before they even got to the real action of Mount Everest. Ever felt overwhelmed? Jim felt the task at hand was insurmountable, but understanding that he had reached a plateau in his life, there was literally no turning back. ***In his own mind, he broke the 120-mile route into bite-sized pieces and focused on them one step at a time.*** He viewed his trek as evolving from a hike to a climb and reflected on personal success in his past where he broke the whole apart to understand the elements.

"The true wisdom is to be always seasonable, and to change with a good grace in changing circumstances."

—ROBERT LOUIS STEVENSON

LESSON TWO:

You can't go full tilt all the time.

Considering that life lessons are a part of your ongoing training, understand that different stages of your life require new acclimatizing. ***Always pace yourself for change and know when to take breaks.*** For Jim, the Mount Everest experience meant a reduction in air pressure and oxygen which generally leads to disorientation, confusion, lack of coordination and a possible fatal fall.

Like Jim, you can push yourself to go farther and faster, but not if you are unused to the climate. And that climate may mean a new job, marriage, stepchildren and everything else that life throws at you.

Understanding your core values will help you make decisions easier.

In life and death situations, your core values (what means the most to you) will become vividly clear. Pulmonary edema and cerebral edema, caused by reduced oxygen and air pressure in the lungs and brain, are two of the most life-threatening illnesses facing climbers of Mount Everest. Jim was faced with his own limits, controlling his own destiny, and considered the loss of his own life in this metaphorical journey. We all face different choices like this, both big and small. **The critical learning is what can we observe from others in order to build upon that wisdom and optimize joy along our path.**

If you don't plan on having a mountain-top epiphany, at least take some advice and take it at your own pace. **Seek to understand your individual core values so you can gauge your own contentment and happiness.**

Consider your own trek and the value system that comes from within, but also understand how your values evolve with time. While simple in nature, your core may be dialed down to faith, family and fun, but your cafeteria of values could extend to:

Advancement at work, authority, cause, community involvement, community of faith, creativity, control of your destiny, gracefulness, family, faith, financial independence, fitness, integrity, leadership, leisure time, personal growth, personal reputation, prestige, responsibility, security, tithing, tradition, travel, variety & diversity.

Draw from this list of core values or add to it, but use it as your life lessons dashboard. Relate each new lesson, each new curve in the road and each new undertaking, against the dashboard.

Life Lesson…

Above all else:

Realize that true success is the
attainment of purpose without
compromising your

CORE VALUES.

CYCLING
THROUGH
ADVERSITIES

Life is full of accidental lessons.

Sue Lundgren, a young, athletic friend from Boulder, Colorado suffered a very serious bicycle accident. With broken ribs, collarbone, and wrist, coupled with a fractured pelvis, Sue was hurting in ALL extremities. The accident required a very painful recovery process with many months of confinement in bed.

When the doctor had completed her work and was taking her leave, Sue asked, "Doctor, how long shall I have to lie here helpless?" ***"Oh, only one day at a time,"*** was the positive answer. The long-suffering patient was not only comforted for the moment, but many times during the succeeding weeks did the thought "only one day at a time" come back with its quieting influence.

Only one day…what if we could teach our children to use each day more effectively with a new perspective on time? In our rapid world, can we teach our families, our communities and the nation to be quick to listen and slow to anger?

> "Comfort and prosperity have never enriched the world as much as adversity has."
> — BILLY GRAHAM

Teaching patience starts by exhibiting a little more patience ourselves. Like Sue Lundgren, we can learn that the soul of perseverance cannot be beaten. The patience she exhibited to her family and friends stands out as a testimony of patience and overcoming adversity. In record time, Sue was back to life, working her way out of adversity. Hard challenges were put in her way, not to stop her, but to call out her courage and strength.

> "The measure of a woman is the way she bears up under misfortune."
> — PLUTARCH

Life Lesson…

Above all else:

Out of difficulty and adversity grows
a more patient and wise person. With a
little patience and a lot of tenacity,
obstacles cannot stop you. And remember,

A GREAT PLEASURE IN LIFE
IS DOING WHAT PEOPLE SAY
YOU CANNOT DO.

DON'T LET THE
PARADE
PASS YOU BY

*"Your sacred space is where you can
find yourself again and again."*

— JOSEPH CAMPBELL

On a pleasant warm June 13th in Manhattan, a young and curious six-year-old, stopped playing for a few moments, pulled up a soap box and gazed over the heads of the onlookers to watch a parade. A former air mail pilot named Charles was being ushered down the street to the applause of many New Yorkers. Parade units included local bands, the police department, the U.S. Calvary and even Boy Scout troops. As Charles' car got closer, the young boy could hear:

"Clap hands, here comes Charlie, clap hands."

A line of school girls was forming down the street creating a "Lindy" in honor of the special guest. In that moment, Charles Pecorera never let a parade pass him by…especially not the one which celebrated another Charles…that of Charles Lindbergh, who had just crossed the Atlantic

Ocean on the first trans-Atlantic flight ever achieved between New York and Paris.

Experience all that life has to offer…don't let the parade pass you by. Be the positive spark in others' lives…get out there and live in the moment.

Rise beautifully to the challenges that life brings you. Be ambitious, come out of your cocoon and take flight.

Charles Pecorera took in all the life and music he could. Starting at age 12, he began playing guitar. His dad, a noted Sicilian guitarist and orchestra musician, taught him basic chords in the first position. Charles went on to learn the second and third positions and all the rest on his own. As he says, "God hands out gifts to people and He gave me the ear for music."

The gift started with great listening skills. Exposed to vaudeville from his dad, he worked "the circuit" in New York City with his dad, frequently playing Jewish theatres, speakeasies and hotels which offered dinner and dancing. During the Prohibition Era, Charles and his dad played at New York's high society speakeasies, often located in the back of fine restaurants. There were secretive passages to clandestine clubs and great music was always played.

His dad also gave him the courage to jump into the parade and perform in a quality manner. Surprising Charles one day, his dad told him to go pick up his new guitar at 40 Kenmore Street. Created for him by Manhattan's famous John D'Angelico, his guitar was custom made with Old World techniques. *Charles had a treasure in his guitar—designed in scale length with a custom neck and body width. Now the young guitarist of extraordinary quality had an extraordinary D'Angelico instrument to match his talent.*

While Charles regrets not finishing school, life's parade didn't pass him by. He accepted offers to play with famous trios and orchestras ranging from Jose Melis to Woody Herman. Jose was a classically-trained pianist who helped pioneer the broadcasting genre as orchestra leader on *The Tonight Show*. He auditioned Charles with great rigor. Handing him the

"When the parade passes by, listen and hear the brass harmony growing, When the parade passes by, pardon me if my old spirit is showing, all of those lights over there, seem to be telling me where I'm going."

— FROM *HELLO, DOLLY!*

sheet music to several classic 1940s songs, Charles retorted with, "That's okay, I know that music." ***Charles had heard it once and could play the guitar part. He had the gift.***

As he matured musically, Charles was often asked to accompany well-known singers. Usually reserved for a pianist, he found himself in the unique position of backing up the best in the industry on Cole Porter classics such as *Night and Day* or *I Get a Kick Out of You*.

Later in life, Charles continued by working for Frank Sinatra at his Beverly Hills' restaurant, Puccini's. He had the rare occasion of serving World Heavyweight Boxing Champion Rocky Marciano and actually introduced him to Sinatra.

Now with a talented son of his own, Charles takes special pride in passing on his great attitude, optimism and musical skills. Charlie Jr. represents the continuous joy that Charles Sr. has sustained and lived. He embodies the same spirit of, "I've gotta get in step while there's still time left, I'm ready to move out in front, life without life has no reason or rhyme left, with the rest of them, with the best of them…before the parade passes by."

For Charles, he never let a parade pass him by. Today, at age 91, he continues to enjoy everything that life offers. ***He has the gift.***

Life Lesson...

Above all else:

In life, find

CONTINUOUS AND INTERESTING

JOY.

Life's Lesson # **8**

DO WHAT
YOU LIKE,
LIKE WHAT
YOU DO

"Go, lovely rose...
Tell her that wastes her time and me
That now she knows,
When I resemble her to thee,
How sweet and fair she seems to be."
— EDMUND WALLER

*B*orn to Italian-American Frank Mazzetta and Polish-American Stella Gluszeak, a three-year-old musical prodigy rose to the occasion at a talent show and became an overnight singing sensation. Armed with the voice of a 25-year-old professionally trained vocalist, this tiny wonder wore a black hair bow and had the stage presence that held three U.S. presidents spellbound.

There she stood in front of Calvin Coolidge, impressing him with an unforgettable American spirit. As a nation plunged into its darkest days of depression following the stock market crash, she brought some hope to Herbert Hoover. For Franklin Delano Roosevelt, the young charmer represented a brighter future and a generation that had higher hopes for a nation that had to pull itself up by its bootstraps. **She was in the "zone" then and remains that way 85 years later!**

"She could punctuate a phrase with a lusty growl

Her lesson was learned early on. Love what you do, love your audience and keep delivering quality entertainment. Why else would audiences keep saying, **"let the kid sing."** One writer commented, "She could punctuate a phrase with a lusty growl that would be remarkable in a singer twice her age."

Her popular voice and upbeat attitude started to reach America on a coast-to-coast basis when NBC signed her as a radio show star. Billed as **"The Darling of the Airwaves,"** this musical initiative was bold, but timely. From this child's talent, America's attention momentarily shifted away from the sadness and job loss of the 1930s to enjoy the sounds of a happy-go-lucky kid from New York.

Years later, a few notorious businessmen pooled their money together to build a hotel and casino in a desolate, deserted part of Nevada. They

"...that would be remarkable in a singer twice her age."

invited the entertaining singer as the opening act, along with Jimmy Durante and the Xavier Cugat Band. With her trademark hair bow in place, the show opened with a full house of Hollywood celebrities including Clark Gable and other stars of the day.

Fast forward to 2007 when the Smithsonian Institution opens a new exhibit wing on the culture of American entertainment. One of eight women chosen for the prestigious honor has a black hair bow enshrined along with the sheet music sung on her radio show.

For that unforgettable voice you know as Sally Rogers from the *Dick Van Dyke Show* and a 14-year regular on *Hollywood Squares*, Rose Marie is now in her 85th year of show business. Asked why she doesn't start another career…

"What else would I do? It's what I know best."

For Rose Marie, she does what she loves to do, and loves what she does. She is profoundly passionate about entertaining and fearless in the face of any audience, even if it was Presidents Coolidge, Hoover, and Roosevelt.

Life Lesson…

Above all else:

LOVE WHAT YOU DO IN LIFE.

For your audience of one
or a hundred, always

LET YOUR PASSION
SHOW THROUGH.

Life's Lesson # **9**

TRANSFORMED BY
TRAVEL

"The real voyage of discovery consists not in seeking new landscapes but in having new eyes."

— MARCEL PROUST

As a child, we vacationed frequently by making a trek from Sherman, Texas, to Fredrickstown, Pennsylvania, visiting my mother's mother and dad, her sister and brother and cousins by the dozens. Along the way, we drove through America's heartland cities, stopped at numerous antique stores on our journey and literally breathed in some of the best of what this country has to offer in terms of people.

For my parents, the big lesson from experiential travel was,

"To be informed is to be transformed."

Today, travel is considered the single most transformative activity in our lives. The intersection of what we know, where we have been and how we observe the comings and goings of each city is in one word…spectacular.

Driving across America meant the first glance of the Arch in St. Louis. We were transformed with the notion that this was THE gateway to the west. Now 40 years later and with a whole lot more empathy for pioneers, a Horace Greeley statue proclaiming "go west young man" would have made more sense.

And speaking of the west, the career aspirations and chase for blissfulness by our two daughters brought them to the enigmatic community of Los Angeles. Lessons are plentiful in this City of Angels, but through the lessons of transformative travel, the essence of this city is worthy of sharing.

As writer Verlyn Klinkenberg observed, *"Something escapes me about Los Angeles."* For the first time visitor, it is a mammoth of concrete highways, a sprawling uber-urban center that has mysterious, magnetic arms that draw in highly ambitious children.

It is the capital for storytelling, in an industry called film and television. And oh, the stories they spin about the *"chance for stardom"* and the *"opportunity of a lifetime."*

The transformative truth of the matter is that you have to earn your way into tinsel town. *The earning takes longer than most industries and the pay along the way is substandard, but oh, the chase of blissfulness is like the siren of the sea.* The seductiveness of the city and its best-known industry is alluring and a time-tested laboratory for those with persistence.

Just like the Arch of St. Louis, one will get a iconic glimpse of LA. It's the sudden view of the Hollywood sign as you get on the 101 Freeway, not the less defined downtown that stands for banking and business institutions.

Follow Route 66 into Pasadena for a transformative moment. Stop, look and listen for the hot rods and Harleys rolling down the road. Close your eyes and imagine a more rebellious era when kids made "the drag" and revved up their engines to impress. It is intensely nostalgic, full of story and worthy of stopping to talk to locals. The hard lesson learned is that you will miss so much, by not engaging with those you meet.

ROUTE US 66

If you can learn to ask the right questions of strangers, they will not be strangers for long.

You can always ask this… ***"Besides yourself, who is the most famous person to ever walk through your store?"*** Eighty percent of the time, you will listen to a remarkable story…one that you will retell to friends and family as you recall your experience in a scrapbook or on your Facebook album.

You can view parts of Hollywood as a city of extraordinary facades, without insinuating that it is a superficial community. Tour the local film studios and you see false fronts, but it is art, just like the actors. Look beyond the facades to an industry that relies on authentic looks to entertain. Recall with fond memories, the talented set artists that preceded the computer graphic artists of today. ***In the heart of set artists was the ability to not only draw but to draw us in.*** Just picture the Land of Oz and you get it.

Life Lesson...

Above all else:

Ask yourself this question about any transformative travel.

IF YOU HAD A LIFETIME TO LIVE, WOULD YOU LIVE PART OF IT IN THE LOCALE YOU ARE VISITING?

Draw life lessons from each new travel experience.

Life's Lesson # **10**

VINTAGE
YEARS

*"I would feel more optimistic about a bright future
for man if he spent less time proving that he can
outwit nature and more time tasting her sweetness
and respecting her seniority."*

— E.B. WHITE 1899-1985

Vintage years are often linked to a wine of a particular type or region that is typically of superior quality. The product is allowed to mature. Connoisseurs and collectors then extend their voice of approval and further build up its importance.

Bill Mumy, actor and musician is "vintage out loud." From 1957 to the present, Bill has worked on hundreds of television shows permanently imprinting his talents on America's culture as an enduring, recognized and quality performer. Bill's approach to recreating and repeating vintage years is as classical as the workmanship of a fine-crafted Les Paul guitar. At his roots is an insistence on quality first, distinction, and building layers of constant improvement. His drive for excellence runs deep and his sounds reflect vintage passion. His appeal is about originality as well as drawing from the vintage years.

Being vintage means building positive layers of experience to produce high-quality work, engaging with a diversity of people to broaden your point of view, and allowing a creative muse to play a role in reinventing yourself. It's about giving yourself permission to grow in a vintage mindset to enjoy life more richly.

Born in San Gabriel, California, in 1954 of notable Hollywood lineage, Bill's grandfather, Harry Gould, was the agent who launched the legendary Boris Karloff into the role of a lifetime as Frankenstein. Having broken his arm as a youngster, Bill watched his share of television. His sense of adventure was heightened by watching George Reeves as Superman and Guy Williams portraying Zorro. At four, he told his parents, Muriel and Charles, that he wanted to be in the adventure of television.

"Vintage Years" start with the long view of looking at your body of work. In Bill Mumy's journey, he has amassed 400 television shows, 18 motion pictures, scores of albums that he has written and performed, and voice over work in animation, narration, and hundreds of television commercials. Each performance was a new floor to build upon. Each is distinctively different, but was done in a consistent, quality manner.

Understand that each layer of experience adds to the vintage body of work. While you may be in the midst of a less fulfilling career, consider the vintage point of view that you are growing and sharpening your skills along the way.

While the world remembers Bill from his role as Will Robinson from *Lost in Space*, his vintage approach was indelibly shaped by working with Rod Serling in *The Twilight Zone*. From 1959-1964, he played in two of television's all-time most popular drama episodes. Starting in March 1961 with "Long Distance Call" as the character Billy Bayles, Mumy was the infamous boy who talked to his dead grandmother through his toy telephone. In November 1961, Bill portrayed a child who terrorizes a town with his psychic powers in "It's a Good Life." Serling also cast him in a seminal 1963 episode titled, "In Praise of Pip" about a little boy name Pip and his relationship with his father.

Turning down opportunities can also be defining as well.

Mumy was the director's choice to play Eddie Munster in the 1964 television series *The Munsters*. While his parents purportedly objected to too much make up, the role may have typecast him for the balance of his career.

At 11-years-old, Bill took his guitar on set to the production of *Lost in Space*. Ironically, Bill's television father was Guy Williams of *Zorro* fame. Leaning against a foam rubber rock formation near the Jupiter II, he played and sang the traditional folk song "Greensleeves" on his guitar for the pilot that launched the series and again for the episode named "Pirate." Even then he was building the vintage approach to creating a notable body of work.

Allowing yourself to engage with others is a defining part of vintage thinking.

Being distinctively vintage, means allowing yourself to be influenced by vintage voices. It means being open to a variety of influences from teachers, supervisors, colleagues, and in Bill's case directors, writers, and fellow actors such as Jonathan Harris who portrayed Dr. Smith on *Lost in Space*. Classic vintage careers will always be influenced by classically-trained professionals. Such was the case with Jonathan and Bill.

Long after they finished their roles as Dr. Smith and young Will Robinson, the two became very good friends, with Jonathan's ***"oh the pain" and "my dear boy" wisdom shaping his thinking.*** The relationship between their families blossomed because they took time to nurture it. Long, quality conversations over dinner had enormous influence on Bill. Simply put, vintage thinking takes time and authentic relationships with classic friends are a vital ingredient.

Likewise in music, vintage sounds and tastes were formulated by working with the popular band *America* as a songwriter and performer, touring as guitarist for Shaun Cassidy, and executing the role as a musician in *Hard to Hold*, a movie that features Rick Springfield's band.

Vintage Years are about reinventing yourself.

Bill Mumy's blues and jazz are great examples. Hearing a certain rhythm from the past, layering it with a new sound, and a 1940s style is quintessential vintage style. It is a fusion of past, present and future creating new ideas, new voices, and new sounds that define vintage.

Life Lesson…

Above all else:

Recognize how your style is being shaped and formed along your journey intentionally sculpting your own vintage style.

ALLOW YOURSELF TO BE POSITIVELY INFLUENCED BY DIVERSITY.

Listen, be fluid and constantly layer your experiences for Vintage Years.

Life's Lesson # **11**

THE
LESSON OF
MINDFULNESS

"Savor it and take it all in.
You will never get that moment back."

— CARLA TOCQUIGNY

We tend to live in the future, not in the present. While growing up, you couldn't wait until you finished elementary school, middle or high school. Or you were anxious to drive your own car and truly experience freedom. When we finally have "it," we want the next best thing. What's on your list for the constantly discontented—a bigger house, a shiny new car, or the latest invention from Apple? Are we not capable of being alive and content in the present moment?

Voices of wisdom often keep us in check with the present. **Mother always said, "Be in the moment."** While on vacation, Mom thoroughly enjoyed different food, the energy of a new city and the artsy feeling of a street festival with local artisans. She proclaimed, "Don't think about your next trip while you are in the middle of a foreign country. Get lost in the smells, sounds and tastes of your whereabouts. Be aware of the here and now and recognize that the only moment to be alive is in the present."

Mindfulness is a terrible thing to waste. If mindfulness is not your traveling companion either, test yourself the next time you see a beautiful sunrise or sunset. **Can you stand still for a few minutes and watch our**

"Let happiness catch you." —ANGELA CARTWRIGHT

Creator's artistic skills at work? Happiness and peace are blaring in your face. Tranquility and beauty are there for you to behold.

In 2009, it happened. Mindfulness traveled with me to Italy. Packing a sketchpad and pencil, I sauntered into the Academia, and did a stare down with Michelangelo's statue of David.

Looking for happiness in front of my face and not in the future, I sat in front of a masterpiece and doodled. Flowing clockwise around David, finding a seat to get a better view, I drew every detail of Michelangelo's creation. I had never noticed all the details because I was never in the moment.

Travelers and art enthusiasts would look over my shoulder, some admiring the sketch and others wondering if this old artist would make the grade in art school.

The moment was transforming and humbling. Time stopped. Mindfulness was liberating, youthful and blew away all preoccupations. The mindfulness pilot light had been lit and has become an eternal light.

What lay ahead was yet to be seen. **Finding oneself in a moment and saying, "hello sir and welcome back" was a moment of grace, joy, euphoria, and epiphany.** How do you live out your life with mindfulness, and remember to BE IN THE PRESENT?

Life Lesson...

Above all else:

Be in the moment, enjoy the
present; take it all in.
Make affirmative comments to
capture each unique window
of time such as

"THERE IS NOTHING QUITE
LIKE THIS VERY MOMENT."

Life's Lesson # **12**

THE LESSON OF
STANDING
STILL

Today's Homework

> *"My success, part of it certainly, is that I have focused in on a few things."*
>
> — BILL GATES

Doug Lemov, a 42-year-old teacher, like many other educators, is always striving to be an effective teacher. Looking like an offensive lineman with a "Beaver Cleaver" face, Doug struggled in his first year of teaching. As he started his new position, nothing quite prepared him for class management, certainly not the student teacher gig.

When Doug conducted his own research on teaching methodologies, he came across too many examples of teachers who were not prepared for their profession. He also discovered a logical and simple mistake being made by teachers.

A Boston teacher advised Doug to, **"stand still when you are giving directions."** In other words, don't do two things at once. Lemov tried it and suddenly, he had to ask students to take out their homework only once.

While it was such a minute change, it made a monumental difference. And when Doug was focused on one thing—one direction, the class responded by following that direction.

Today, many mistakes are driven by multi-tasking. When we sit still and listen, we improve our retention of information and our quality of work.

Remember learning...

+ *Whenever possible, do one thing at a time.*
+ *"Be still, and know that I am God." Psalm 46:10 NIV*
+ *Don't change radio stations as you are driving, much less talk on your phone or text. Have you seen the movie "Seven Pounds?"*
+ *Instead of trying to plan every little detail of life, dive into the present moment tapping into your intuitive, internal guidance system.*
+ *Look, stand still and really see.*
+ *Practice dropping everything for a moment of focus.*
+ *Get up earlier, give yourself quiet time. Use this habit to build your ability to be singular in your focus.*
+ *Build the mental capability to listen to your intellect, experience and intuition.*

Life Lesson…

Above all else:

Pause and savor ideas,
concepts, pictures and sensations
to make yourself fully alive.

PRACTICE THIS AS YOU LIVE YOUR LIFE.

(CONSIDER THESE A GIFT, NOT A DISTRACTION.)

Life's Lesson # **13**

LISTEN AND
TRUST
IN YOUR
INNER VOICE

"The best career advice to give to the young is to find out what you like doing best and get someone to pay you for doing it."

— KATHERINE WHITEHORN

*I*n the first grade, our tall, red-headed teacher, Cleo Reagan, asked us…"How many artists are in this class?" We all raised our hands. Four years later, our short, diminutive art instructor, Wanda Helvey, asked the same question and only one-third of the same class responded by raising their hands.

By the seventh grade we were down to one-sixth of the class and finally by our senior year, only two out of the original 25 raised their hands. What happened across twelve years? Had we been sucker punched with self-doubt about our artistic abilities?

At the start of our schooling, our parents gave frequent positive feedback about our artwork as they proudly displayed our renderings on the refrigerator. Somewhere along the path of our elementary education, some person or teacher pointed out a mistake and we started focusing on those comments. The presumed mistakes manifested themselves into, "I can't draw, I'm not an artist." We internalized the criticism and forever gave up on some of the best talent that 2-to 5-year-old children had developed. The majority of artists started listening to other voices and putting more credence in the opinion of their peers versus their own inner voice of confidence. *Who has the right to feed you such negativity?*

The mistake made is in listening to other people. On top of that, the grading process of the arts is questionable. Grading systems point out flaws. Isn't the whole idea of school to learn, grow and become a contributing citizen?

"Be who you are and say what you feel because those who mind don't matter and those who matter don't mind."

— DR. SEUSS

Life Lesson...

Above all else:

Listen to your inner voice
and have confidence that you can

CHASE YOUR OWN PASSION.

Foster an intimacy with your own
skills and confidently build from
your first level of success.

Life's Lesson # **14**

RIGHT TIME,
RIGHT
PLACE

Even If It's Over the Hill time

"I will prepare and some day my chance will come."
— ABRAHAM LINCOLN

$\mathcal{S}$ome people are repeatedly in the right place at the right time. Never chalking it up to dumb luck, good fortune is closely linked with hard-working people who have the smarts to position themselves for success. While some may concede that it is destiny, rarely will you find a lazy person making remarkable discoveries. ***Truly, the secret of success in life goes to the man or woman ready for the opportunity when he or she faces it.***

Novel discoveries often happen because of curiosity and sheer enthusiasm. With a consistent, inquisitive mind, discoverers position themselves to be in that right vertical slice called ***opportunity.***

By always moving toward the next opportunity, Allan Shook put himself squarely in the right place and right time.

As a product inventor and consumer guru fascinated with why people buy products, he made it a habit to look, ask questions and listen.

In April of 1981, while serving as vice president of a small, independent greeting card chain of stores, Allan was engaged with the owner's sons to start manufacturing gifts and stationery. During a visit to one of the stores, Allan noticed a middle-aged woman (Judy) in the party section. She had her arms full of party goods and clearly needed an extra hand. Shook jumped right in and asked her if he could help, and Judy was grateful for the assistance.

With all the store clerks busy, Allan took over the check-out process for Judy and he began to notice something quite odd about her purchase. Why was she buying cartloads of black napkins and black party plates in April? These were generally purchased in October for Halloween parties.

As Allan's curiosity peaked, he inquired, "May I ask you something? *Why are you buying so many black party supplies in April?*" Judy chuckled and explained that her husband Bob was turning 40, and was quite depressed about the upcoming event. To mourn the passing of Bob's youth, Judy was engineering an old-fashioned wake around this 40th birthday milestone. Dressed in black, all the party-goers would eulogize Bob and place their fond words into a rented coffin. Allan had never heard a more enthusiastic shopper getting ready for a party!

For Allan Shook, it was one of those "moments in time." ***While most would have simply moved on with their day, something inside Allan moved him to act.*** Making a quick phone call to one of the company owners, the two decided to complete a little research on the aging population of America.

In a matter of hours, Allan and his crew became informed and amazed that over 80 million Americans were going to be turning 40 and then 50. Judy was not one of a kind, but the tip of the iceberg for a trend that could last for the next 30+ years.

With the trade show season upon them, Allan's team went to work and within three weeks ***invented and displayed five gift and party items in the now***

infamous "Over the Hill" theme. In one weekend, his team wrote orders exceeding $30,000! They rushed to get the products manufactured, shipped and delivered to their stores. As a product pioneer, Allan eventually invented over one hundred separate items that led to a multi-million dollar corporation.

While Thomas Jefferson may be credited as coining "Over the Hill," ***Allan Shook is credited with introducing these theme products into the social expression industry.*** Eventually, his company sold for a handsome price as its value soared on this singular idea.

For Shook, luck was never under his control, but location and timing were. Allan's one-minute interaction with Judy began the "Over the Hill" craze that swept the world.

"Talent alone won't make you a success.
Neither will being at the right place and right time,
unless you're ready. The most important question is:

Are you ready?"

— JOHNNY CARSON

Life Lesson…

Above all else:

If you are truly willing to work hard enough and smart enough to get where you've always dreamed of going,

YOUR RIGHT PLACE AND RIGHT TIME ARE CLOSER THAN EVER,

especially if you keep an inquisitive edge. Extraordinary things do happen in life.

Life's Lesson # **15**

ROSES AND
THORNS

"Don't be afraid to fail. Don't waste energy trying to cover up failure. Learn from your failures and go on to the next challenge. It's OK to fail. If you're not failing, you're not growing."

— H. STANLEY JUDD

Reunion Tower is one of the signature structures of the Dallas, Texas skyline offering tourists and locals beautiful views of the "DFW Metroplex." Designed in 1977 by Welton Becket and Associates from Los Angeles, California, Reunion is the 15th tallest structure in the downtown area towering 560 feet.

Gary Coffman worked on the construction of the tower from the beginning to its debut in 1978. *Like a beautiful rose rising from the earth, the tower had its share of thorns. As a matter of fact, the construction of this iconic tower led to a lessons-learning process used within Gary's firm called "Roses & Thorns."*

Any visitor to Dallas can tell you about Reunion Tower's light show. It has become a symbolic part of the city, celebrating each holiday, big event, and sports championship.

Reunion has taken on its own personality to resemble the "best of times" the city has to offer. With construction of this "rose" came a good dose of "thorns." Consider that the shaft of the tower is constructed from poured-in-place concrete featuring four mammoth concrete cylinders. Three are placed on the outside in a triangular pattern housing elevators that offer passengers a beautiful view as they ride up and down. The center cylinder houses stairs and mechanical shafts.

The top of Reunion is a three-level structure, also constructed of poured-in-place concrete surrounded at the top by a geodesic dome formed by aluminum struts. At the intersection of the aluminum members are 260 lights that are turned on for the Reunion Tower signature light shows.

Elegantly designed with great function, Gary worked on the completion of three levels at the top. **The lowest level is known as The Lookout, with an observation deck.** Offering a 360-degree walk that is covered by the upper levels, one can see Oklahoma on a clear day to the North and vast prairies to the West. **The second level houses Antares, a revolving, full-service restaurant. The third deck is The Dome, a contemporary cocktail lounge that also makes a complete revolution every 55 minutes.**

Understanding that construction is an imperfect science, Gary's company experienced an unfortunate outcome when the 260 lights on one side of the tower went out. Rigid enough vibration and tolerance tests were not completed to understand the motion effect on the filaments of the 260 bulbs. One could reason that if the bulbs used were from a battleship that withstood the firing of artillery, they would surely handle Reunion Tower on its busiest day.

Adopting a positive approach to "fluid" problem solving, his team created a "roses and thorns" session that had architects, engineers and construction supervisors openly discussing issues and answers about the construction process. They recognized that construction "miss-takes" were going to occur.

The object of the game became—how do we minimize error, anticipate issues and fix them along the patch of the project completion?

Using the "roses and thorns" process, Gary's teams kept projects flowing. According to Gary, "We now have a debriefing process built into projects. *While most learning experiences are in our head, 'roses and thorns' brings the information forward. Why let 'miss-takes' embroil in the minds of your colleagues?"*

Massive projects like Reunion Tower require huge amounts of resources. At our company, I don't want my team to feel frozen with fear and flawing the process. If we spanked people every time a construction "miss-take" is made, our paddle would be broken. As a result of this positive approach, the average company employee has over 21 years of tenure in a 38-year-old organization.

In the end, the "roses and thorns" process fixed the lighting issues by using a special light bulb that could tolerate vibration. The bulbs were sourced from traffic lights with filaments that were constructed to withstand severe vibration. The light show now goes on… to the delight of millions.

Life Lesson…

Above all else:

Adopt your own "roses and thorns" process to check quality and ensure excellence along the path of any project. Insist on open communication and "no penalty boxes" for acknowledging "miss-takes." Great communication is a great stabilizer unto itself.

DON'T BE AFRAID TO FAIL.

Don't waste energy trying to cover up failure. Learn from your failures and move on to the next challenge.

Life's Lesson #

NATURALLY

"You can't be afraid to make errors!
You can't be afraid to be naked before the crowd,
because no one can ever master the game of baseball,
or conquer it. You can only challenge it."

— LOU BROCK

*T*ed Waitkus was 29 years old when his dad's story was immortalized in the movie, *The Natural.* Until then he was simply known as a humble man who endured great tragedy and triumph in his 52 years. But, as is usually the case, there is more to his story than was told on the silver screen. This is what Ted knew of the man, as a soldier, a father, and a baseball legend:

Edward Stephen Waitkus was born September 4th, 1919, to Lithuanian immigrants in Cambridge, Massachusetts. He grew up in a solid family amidst the financial turmoil of the Great Depression and eventually turned down scholarships to Harvard University and Holy Cross to play baseball. Being a student didn't pay the bills. Playing baseball did.

Like many young men during his day, he was drafted to fight in World War II. Eddie managed to escape combat physically unscathed, but his spirit would never be the same. Those who have seen the horrors of war never sleep that soundly again. By the time he returned to the States, he'd earned three bronze stars and one Silver Star for valor in battle.

Ted often wondered if his biggest loss during the war wasn't his innocence. Eddie Waitkus lost friends. He lost commanders. But it is believed that losing his trust in the basic goodness of man impacted him more deeply than anything else.

After his time in the war, Eddie pursued his first love: baseball. In 1946 he stepped onto the field wearing a Chicago Cubs uniform. In 1948 he was traded to the Philadelphia Athletics. Never a man to pursue anything half-heartedly, Eddie plunged headlong into the game and within a few years earned a reputation as one of the best first-basemen in the world. What he soon learned is that attracting attention to oneself can be fatal.

"A 19-year-old honey with a gun changed my life forever."

That's what he always said and he had a lot of time to reflect on his decision in the years that followed. At the time, it seemed perfectly reasonable to go to her hotel room.

On June 14th, 1949, the Philadelphia A's played the Cubs in Chicago. Just as they had done in the past, the team stayed at the Edgewater Beach Hotel. At the time Eddie was dating a young woman named Ruth and she would often visit him on the road. So when he got back to the hotel after the game and received a note at the front desk saying, **"Ruth is waiting for you in room 215,"** *he didn't question it.*

Eddie walked up to her room as naively as he walked on the battlefields of Europe. What he found behind that door was a similar fate. Instead of the kind, young woman he'd been dating, he found a deranged fan with a .22 rifle. **As soon as he entered the room she fired a single shot to the chest.**

Mental illness was a taboo subject in those days. It was treated discreetly, and often unaffectedly, but rarely diagnosed in advance. For Ruth Ann Steinhagen, her growing obsession with Eddie Waitkus had simply been ignored. Whether or not her family was troubled by the fact that she set a place for him at the dinner table each night or had erected

a shrine in his honor at the foot of her bed, was never known. Perhaps because she was so young it was simply passed off as an innocent fancy. But there was nothing innocent about her intentions in that hotel room. When questioned by the police later, Ruth Ann simply shrugged and said, **"If I can't be with Eddie, neither can other women."**

They'd never even met before. Yet the fact that he was in a relationship with another woman enraged Ruth Ann to the point of murder. She almost succeeded.

The bullet entered his chest cleanly and missed his lung by a fraction of an inch. But it left a much bigger mess on the way out, blowing a hole almost three inches wide in his back. Surgeons were not able to patch it together cleanly and the result was the large pock-marked scar that fascinated me so much as a child.

Eddie told this story to his son Ted with surprising clarity. He remembered those few moments he spent with Ruth Ann Steinhagen, her cold eyes staring at him as he struggled to breathe. And that could have been the end had she not picked up the phone and called the police to confess what she'd done. Emergency medical help arrived just in time. They rushed him to the nearest hospital where he underwent emergency surgery to stop the hemorrhaging. He died on the operating room table three times during the procedure and each time doctors were able to bring him back. **Eddie Waitkus would go on to defy the odds and make a full recovery.** As for Ruth Ann Steinhagen, she went to a mental institution for three years and was then released with no further consequences.

"I've often wondered if that bullet she placed in my father's chest didn't raise up the lingering emotions from his time in the military," says Ted. Eddie had seen the horrors of war first hand, yet it was on foreign soil, done at the hands of strange men with slanted eyes. But now he stood on home ground and had seen the reality that violence and obsession were possible anywhere. As any remaining trust in people melted away, my father retreated inward. He was a different man. **The combination of his war experiences started to take hold of his confidence on and off the field.**

Perhaps as a way to escape his inner demons, he threw himself into physical therapy so he could return to the game. One year later he found himself in Florida for training. It was there that he found reason to hope in the form of a young woman. She would later become Ted's mom.

That year turned out to be one of the most significant of his life. **Not only did he meet and marry the love of his life, but he returned to the game that had given him so much.** Eddie Waitkus and the Philadelphia A's won the pennant in the last game of the season. He scored the winning run. They then went on to win the World Series. It was a high he couldn't top and ultimately, the beginning of the lowest part of his life.

All athletes age, and all good things come to an end. The baseball career of Eddie Waitkus wound to a close. Yet he was never able to adjust to life outside of the game. He'd spent his entire adult life on the field with a bat in his hand and had nothing else to fall back on. When he retired, he traded the bat for some vices he would regret.

Ted often wondered how his mother dealt with the transformation. She married a carefree romantic in sunny Florida and many years later found herself living with a struggling man. They divorced when Ted was 9.

It was only natural for Eddie to end up working for Ted Williams as a batting instructor. It eased the pain of being out of the game and gave him something to focus on after his personal life dissolved. And he loved it. **Perhaps that was the most important thing.**

Some people may look at Eddie Waitkus' life and focus on the things that went wrong. For Ted, he sees a man who truly lived his life and endured the best, and worst, it had to throw at him with his chin held high. He was a man who experienced great tragedy, but still managed to maintain an idealistic outlook on life. He never sought revenge, not on the Japanese soldiers during WWII or on Ruth Ann Steinhagen. A philosophical side emerged as he aged, softening the rougher edges and adding a gentleness that was absent in his early years. He learned to forgive and he refused to harbor hatred.

At the age of 52, Ted's dad checked into the hospital for pneumonia and died a few days later from a cancer no one knew he had. True to his character, Eddie Waitkus went out in an unexpected way and he left a void behind. It's an emptiness that Ted has been trying to fill ever since.

Having spent the greater part of his life sifting through the lessons his father taught him both in word and deed, Ted now realizes that he gave him a sense of identity.

"I am the son of Eddie Waitkus and that has been the foundation upon which I've built my life. I know who I am."

Now in the position to pass the torch to the next generation of Waitkus', Ted looks at his daughter and sees a young woman who doesn't understand these lessons because she has yet to experience adversity. **"Life is different for her than it was for my father, or even for me. She knows the stories, but I want them to become part of the fabric of her life."** We are in part who we are because of where we come from. The blood of Eddie Waitkus runs through her veins.

Ted has lived without the physical presence of his father since he was 17. "When I think about him now, as a man and a father myself, I wish I could play just one more game of catch with him. I wish I could show him all the good he did in my life and how I'm a better man because of it. I wish he knew that the legacy he left me was not a series of scattered mistakes, but a solid foundation of character and admiration."

In the end, Ted has come to understand that the game of life is much like the game of baseball. As Lou Brock says,

"You can't be afraid to make errors! You can't be afraid to be naked before the crowd, because no one can ever master the game of baseball, or conquer it. You can only challenge it."

Eddie Waitkus challenged life. He stepped up to the plate each day, bat-ready, and took what he was given. He had his share of outs, but he also knocked the ball out of the park on more than one occasion. **He wasn't afraid to live and that is more than most can say.**

From his father, Ted learned important lessons in life: decency, acceptance and work ethic. **He also learned that life can be destroyed in a moment and that the world turns over every twenty-four hours.**

Life Lesson...

Above all else:

You may be on bottom today, but just wait.
Tomorrow you can be back on top.

NOTHING IS CERTAIN AND
NOTHING IS FREE.

ABOUT THE AUTHOR

RICK TOCQUIGNY

Rick Tocquigny is CEO and Chief Servant of Artbeat of America and Gracefully Yours Greeting Cards. His time and talents are also spent as an author, publisher, drummer for a 60s band, and host of the popular blog-talk radio show *Life Lessons*. Rick chairs the Procter & Gamble Alumni Network Publishing and Speakers Bureau. He resides in Colorado with his wife, Carla, and can be reached at lifelessonsradio@gmail.com.

If you have enjoyed this book we invite you to check out
our entire collection of gift books with free inspirational movies,
at www.simpletruths.com. You'll discover it's a great way to inspire friends
and family, or to thank your best customers and employees.

FOR MORE INFORMATION, PLEASE VISIT US AT:
WWW.SIMPLETRUTHS.COM OR CALL US TOLL FREE...
800-900-3427